POETRY

In the Blood / *Cortège* / *From the Devotions* / *Pastoral* / *The Tether* / *Rock Harbor* / *The Rest of Love* / *Riding Westward* / *Quiver of Arrows: Selected Poems, 1986–2006* / *Speak Low* / *Double Shadow* / *Silverchest* / *Reconnaissance* / *Wild Is the Wind* / *Star Map with Action Figures* (chapbook) / *Pale Colors in a Tall Field* / *Then the War: And Selected Poems, 2007–2020*

Firsts: 100 Years of Yale Younger Poets (editor) / *Personal Best: Makers on Their Poems That Matter Most* (coeditor with Erin Belieu)

PROSE

Coin of the Realm: Essays on the Life and Art of Poetry / *The Art of Daring: Risk, Restlessness, Imagination* / *My Trade Is Mystery: Seven Meditations from a Life in Writing*

TRANSLATION

Sophocles: *Philoctetes*

Scattered Snows, to the North

Carl Phillips

SCATTERED
SNOWS,
to the
NORTH

FARRAR STRAUS GIROUX

NEW YORK

Farrar, Straus and Giroux
120 Broadway, New York 10271

Illustration on page 55: *The hare in the rain*, by
Tom Knechtel; courtesy of Marc Selwyn Fine Art.

Library of Congress Cataloging-in-Publication Data
Names: Phillips, Carl, 1959– author.
Title: Scattered snows, to the north / Carl Phillips.
Description: First edition. | New York : Farrar, Straus and Giroux, 2024. |
Identifiers: LCCN 2023059595 | ISBN 9780374612412 (hardcover)
Subjects: LCGFT: Poetry.
Classification: LCC PS3566.H476 S33 2024 | DDC 811/.54—dc23/eng/20240108
LC record available at https://lccn.loc.gov/2023059595

Designed by Crisis

Our books may be purchased in bulk for promotional, educational, or business use. Please
contact your local bookseller or the Macmillan Corporate and Premium Sales Department at
1-800-221-7945, extension 5442, or by email at MacmillanSpecialMarkets@macmillan.com.

www.fsgbooks.com
Follow us on social media at @fsgbooks

1 3 5 7 9 10 8 6 4 2

Now let's sit here for a bit, and stop
being sorry about the things we've done.

—TARJEI VESAAS

CONTENTS

SOMEWHERE
IT'S
STILL
SUMMER

REGIME

As I took off
my clothes, I
watched him taking

his own off. The sound
of rain was for
once not the sound

of wind shaking
the rain steadily loose
from a stand

of river birch. It's hard
to believe in them,
the beautiful colors

of extinction; but
these are the colors.

BEFORE ALL OF THIS

And as usual, early summer seems already to hold, inside it,
the split fruit of late fall, those afternoons whose
diminished music we'll soon enough
lie down in—surprised, a little, to feel at all
surprised . . .

      Meanwhile, how the wind sometimes makes
the slenderest trees, still young, bend over

makes me think of knowledge conquering
superstition, I can almost
believe in that—until the trees, like

                    fear, spring back. Then a sad
sort of quiet, just after, as between two people who have finally realized
they've stopped regretting the same things. It's like they've never
known each other. Yet even now, waking, they insist they've woken
from a dream they share, forgetting all over again
that every dream
is private . . .

      Whatever the reasons are for the dead
under-branches of the trees that flourish here, that the dead persist
is enough; for me, it's enough.

The air stirs like history

Like the future

Like history

VIKINGS

The Vikings thought the wind was a god, that the eyes
were holes. A window meant a wind-eye, for the god to see with,
and at the same time through. I used to hate etymology—
What's the point, I'd whisper: I was quieter back then, less
patient, though more easily pleased. I am pleased to have been
of use, I used to say to myself, after sex with strangers. Leaning
hard against the upstairs window, I'd watch them make their half
proud, half ashamed-looking way wherever, and if it was

autumn—whether in fact, or only metaphorically—I'd watch
the yard fill with leaves, then with what I at first thought was
urgency, though it usually turned out just to be ambition. I'd
leave the window open, as I do now—if closed, I open it—
then pull the drapes shut across it, which of the many I've tried
remains the best way I know, still, to catch a wind god breathing.

Maybe what a river loves most
about the banks that hold it—that appear to hold it—
is their willingness or resignation to being
    mere context for the river's progress
or retreat, depending. And maybe how the cattails
and reeds thrive there means they *prefer*
    a river-love—how the river, running always away

the way rivers tend to, stands as proof that reliability
doesn't have to mean steadfast, how the river
    itself would say so, if a river could say . . . I've forgotten
entirely what it felt like to enter his body
    or to be entered by his. But not how he'd spend
long afternoons—as if to look away had become
impossible—just watching his face get routinely

    blurred by the river's motion, like an
inside-out version, psychologically, of a painting
where the model sleeps beneath a portrait
    of himself not sleeping, if that makes
any sense . . . Not, I mean, that he wasn't capable
of love, but that—like history already mistaking itself
    for myth again—he loved a river.

FALL COLORS

I've been looking hard at all my friendships—all of them together,
and each on its own—and although they feel real enough, from what
I can tell, on both sides, I understand now that what they have in common
is a lack of warmth and compassion; who can say at this point why that is,
or how it matters now, if it does. I say I understand it, but it's more true
to say I've *come* to understand it, having had it pointed out to me, for no
reason that I remember, by the only man I think I've ever loved absolutely,
and still do. That's a separate thing. Like my fear of fire. Or like how
much of my time I spend pretending I'm *not* afraid, negotiating this life
with all the seeming casualness with which a man whose business involves
the handling of fires daily

                           daily handles a fire. Some days, it works: I
almost believe myself, or more exactly, and more disturbingly, if I really
think about it (Don't think about it), I almost believe in the self that's just
an imitation of a self I want others to believe in enough for me eventually
to believe it, too. Believing in, versus believing . . . The trumpet vine that grows
up the ginkgo's trunk and has even reached its branches is an example of
instinct, not affection. Twice a day, instead of walking, I take my dog for
what I call a ramble, where each corner we turn feels like a turning, as well,
of imagination. The sun's behind us now; its heat, on this cold November
afternoon that'll soon join all the rest whose details I've forgotten, seems
a small encouragement: all that's needed, most times. I stop; the dog stops—
our shadows, too. They bloom our shadows north-northeast in front of us.

THIS IS THE LIGHT

This is the deep light you've waited for, unfiltered except
now and then by the memory of your first time seeing it,
soon the night-dark after that, filling with sounds that were
strange only from your own mixed perspective as the latest
stranger to have passed through by accident, if there's such
    a thing. Now you live here, where it's likeliest you'll die, too,
you're finally old enough, not just to say, but—without
sorrow or fear, most of the time—to understand the truth of it,
the mind done with signaling, letting its watch fires, one by one,
go out: the renegade glamour of late fall, owlish, fox-ish, how
    brightness is and isn't a color exactly, the one tree from a
city years ago, its weeping branches of pink-white poisonous
berries, like a vow against winter, against giving in, or as if
    the tree, to cover its nakedness, had chosen a stole of what,
when looked at closely, seem the shrunken heads of goblins
in miniature—from afar, just berries, more proof that victory
wears best when worn quietly, or it never happened, or to
someone else, I'm only trying to help you, let me help you,
    he said, something like that, unbuckling; they sailed for hours;
the water that day was as close to perfect as perfect gets here.

ARTILLERY

It's like a habit with you—your idea of tenderness—
leading the blameless a little more blameward just so
you yourself can feel a bit less lonely: In what world
is that tenderness? And though I disagreed with him,

I made no argument, it was that earlyish part of
twilight when it's mostly light, still, above us
the thunderclouds had begun clambering over
the mountains like sluggish bears just done wintering,

I could see, beneath us, a small flock of wild turkeys
in a wilderness that used to be the lawn, back when
I believed in lawns, when suffering still seemed
a thing worth singing about. Why not call it love—

each gesture—if it does love's work? I pulled him
closer. I kissed his mouth, its anger, its blue confusion.

REFRAIN

My fortress has many windows; from this one,
I can tell the tide's going out, I can see the small, purplish flowers,
further up from the water, that you never stopped calling sea thistle,

though that's still not right. The ring of aspens
that surround my fortress, that of course know nothing of east or
west or love when scattered in all its countless definitions,

form a natural palisade that, in leafless months, can seem especially
severe but somehow, as well, inviting, how forgiveness might look
in the face, say, if it had a face, and forgiveness

were real. My fortress is cold and windless; it's a choice,
not to step from it. I believe in gift as much, I think, as I believe
in mastery. Even your mistakes were delicate.

—thin;
aquatic;
moving like an

insistent but gently
reverberating halo of
expectations, kinetic

crown pulled forward,
as if magnetically,
across the ocean's floor.

WHEN WE GET THERE

All day they wandered up and down the shore
against which they'd run their raft
hard aground.
No other people,
no signs of any. Seabirds ranging from
       plovers like soft, mechanical figurines to
ospreys on wings-like-shields descending to pull fish
from the water, but leisurely, as if to hunt were merely
to bloom from one dream to the next aboard a ship called *Love, Persuasion*
—though not a ship
in sight. Water meets shore, the shore gives way
to a double forest, first of blue spruce, then behind
       and towering over it a forest of ginkgos whose fallen leaves like
unexpected hush money lying caught in the spruce trees' boughs
make them look imperial, or like pine trees
in drag. It appears
we're stranded, said the bearded man
to the younger man, who didn't look like he ever even
needed to shave. More like marooned,
       he answered, whereupon they began arguing, about language first,
then about precision: how resistance is only technically
the same thing as hope; the relative
pointlessness of trying to decide, between masochism and sadism,

which is better, when the answer is yes . . . Until soon

it was night. And having no axe, they broke the raft up by hand

for firewood. Then made a fire. Then slept beside it, one holding

    the other, but loosely enough to look

more like apology than anything

more than that, between them. The ginkgo trees

tossed in a wind blowing up off the water;

the spruce trees didn't. The ospreys

slept in their nests, presumably: for omens

also need sleep; indeed, the best ones can sleep for years, uninterrupted.

REHEARSAL

Does it matter that the Roman
Empire was still early in its slow
unwinding into never again? Then,
as now, didn't people burst into tears
in front of other people, or in private,
for no reason that they were willing
to give, or they weren't yet able to,

or for just no reason? I've never
stopped missing you, I used to
practice saying, for when I'd
need those lines, as I assumed
I would, given what I knew then—
nothing, really—about things
like love, trust, the betrayal
of trust, and a willfulness that's
only deepened inside me, all
these years, during which I can
almost say I've missed no one—
though it hurts,
            to say it . . .

Honestly, the Roman Empire,
despite my once having studied it,

barely makes any sense to me now,
past the back-and-forthing of
patrolled borders as the gauge
and proof of hunger's addictive
and erosive powers. But there were
people, of course, too, most of them
destined to be unremembered,
who filled in their drawn lives
anyway—because what else
is there?—to where the edges
gave out. If it was night, they lit
fires, presumably. Tears
were tears.

LITTLE WINTER

Little season, caught, or stranded, between whatever
inside us makes us each go on and the less predictable part,
more fragile, that makes us want to. Little fever-snow of
days when, just as certain colors, even now, can suggest a time
that you called innocent, more honest—though to think so
is itself dishonest, none of it was true, or for only some
was it true—you understand, and can almost admit it,

that the years and energy you've spent forgetting someone
only mean you remember, still: at once more clearly and with
increasing inaccuracy, until what's false, being all you can see,
becomes the past that justifies

                            all the things you are. It's
more than a bit, I think, like that question, If someone
dreams about you, does it keep you alive?—to which
the only good answer is, In the end, will it matter? Just
this morning, what looked like signal fires being lit at random
from the mind's high watchtowers—half-abandoned, now,
but still under guard against siege by barbarians—

turned out instead to be the light reflected off
the blade of a knife that a gloved hand, as if disembodied—

I couldn't *see* a body—had extended, but to no one visible,
with the handle outward, as one does in friendship, or
toward an enemy in truce. Then the hand let go of it. And then
I was the knife, flashing, spinning downward, in a bright, bright sun.

WESTERN EDGE

I need you
the way astonishment,
which is really just

the disruption of routine,
requires routine.
Isn't there

a shock, though—
a thrill—
to having done

what we had to?
Unequally, but
in earnest, we love

as we can,
he used to mumble,
not so much his

mouth moving,
more the words
themselves sort of

staggering around lost
inside it . . . Now
show me

exactly what
you think being brave
is.

SURFERS

Probably this morning's surfers
aren't that much different from the ones I used to watch
nearly fifty years ago, whose glamour seemed
so much more fixed, more absolute from a distance
than when they got
                              too close, which is the fault
not of myth, but of turning people *into* myth. I was
a kid then; and they were, more or less, men,
soon they'd be men for real, meaning,
more or less, boys. They rarely
                              smiled at me. They never
touched me. They mostly pretended not to notice me,
though one time, watching them from where I'd
hidden in a stretch of dune grass, I could see
a couple of them with hands raised to their eyes,
scanning the dunes as if searching, and I stood up,
un-hid myself,
                              and I could tell they'd missed me. Toward
nightfall, I'm a lighthouse, I'm a lighthouse, I'd sing
to myself but very softly, because boys
aren't lighthouses, that's nonsense, repeat
after me. I could never have guessed at it back then, this
second life. It was all I could do, just to be patient

as they paddled their boards out again, into the waves,
then they'd catch one,
                              and flashing my arms—extended
in front of me like the twin beams of light that,
softly, they'd always been also—I'd guide the men in:
to shore, then closer, as if there were a choice that summer
—or ever—and I'd chosen, and I could almost still see it, from here.

WHY SO THIS QUIET

    Dog lifts his leg to piss on the bullbrier; pisses;
and up from the twists and thorns flies a ghost moth,
two of them, three, moving like an abandoned
but still persuasive, still shifting argument,
    until as usual they move how they move, even as
the field's edge means the edge of the field, not
the shadow-stitched perimeter of childhood
    where someone's explaining to me all over again
"A whip is not a lasso," losing patience,
while someone else strikes a match, sets fire
    to a box of maple leaves—desire—"No,
    the leaves are what desire looks like, not how it feels."

HEROIC INTERVAL

Up from the bottom of wherever in the mind things go
to be forgotten, most of them forever, he reappears
at the edge of that meadow inside me I've spent
most of my life trying to convince others isn't made up
at all, but real. As

               he was. Is. Above him, a bewilderment
of black swans pulling their bodies across a band
of nightfall, though it can't be night, for the meadow's
not dark yet, it keeps flashing like a basin of water set down

       *

in sunlight. As he walks towards me, it almost looks
like the routine gesture with interruptions that I
used to think love more or less came down to, before I
figured out I could stop—

               I could always have stopped—
and should maybe try to. Closer, now. He parts the grasses,
breast-high, in front of him. His arms like blades
meant for winnowing intimacy from tenderness, or

       *

nostalgia from truth. Nothing's changed. Still the kind
of man who sees no reason to take his gloves off—

assassin gloves—during sex. Still what feels like a dream
at first, that moment in dream when a friend you've
learned not to trust entirely

                        turns to tell you—

half threatening it, half consolation—the only dream
is this one. But it isn't a dream—I can tell. He'd be
taking his gloves off. He'd be raising his soft hands
to his face—scorched map; busted compass. He'd have a face.

IF GRIEF IS MOSTLY PRIVATE
AND ALWAYS VARIOUS

As for the sea, where's that sound now, that the snow made
in black and white, falling into it, the snow like words from
a severed head held aloft, upside down, and shaken—

> *Nothing can ever/will ever/be the same.*
> *Even if still reckless: wildering;*
> *wild. Though I seem tame.*

SEARCHLIGHTS

All at once, the tiger lilies were out and we'd come too far, world
versus what I've called the world versus what I've made of it
and shaped to my taste, favoring, instead of the sky's edgeless
statement about vastness, the sea's mixed set of questions whose
only answers, finally, are the questions themselves, Is pleasure
in fact a lens to make suffering

                              more legible, for example, Do
betrayal and loyalty share the same mechanism? In my experience
there's not that much difference, usually, between asking and
to have said quite enough. Sometimes a wind demolishes the trees
that were planted, years ago, for stopping the wind, one had come
to rely on them as upon memory, as when we call
our memories proportionate, even remotely, to what was true,
when all we can really say, or maybe should, is This is what
feels true, mostly, when I think of it now,

                                   his face a brokenness
but as a Paleolithic fragment of a reindeer antler decorated
with an image of a horse might, too, be considered a brokenness,
him turning away from then back towards me, I can see my face,
my mouth moving inside it, I can see the words, though I can't
hear them, finding shape first, then meaning, the way smoke does,
Don't, which is not a question; then just the smell of rain, which is.

There are pleasures so ordinary that we barely notice them.
They leave no impression worth mentioning, even. Not
the leaves but the delicate under-leaves that we'd
    somehow missed. Not the stranger whom we've never met,
whom we pass on the walk each morning,
but the matched set of off-white-not-quite-ivory-though
    spaniels that seem to float like two patches of low fog
to either side of him. I used to worry
about the impression I left on others; and then I really
    don't remember which came first: I grew up?
I grew tired? Desire had become by then something different
from what it had been. More hurricane than tornado, its
    damage therefore more easily at least prepared against,
if not forestalled. That certain gestures
don't so much linger as seem to make a routine of
    unexpectedly becoming more apparent some moments
than at others doesn't mean we miss them, means there were parts
that we loved. I regret almost nothing. I come
    in peace A lost beast A crown of feather grass A matching wreath

SOMEWHERE IT'S STILL SUMMER

Here's where they stopped to rest, presumably, this
easy-enough-to-miss depression in the low-cut grass. I like
to think they had a chance to sleep a bit, before
    everything else, all the rest that followed, that they neither
        deserved nor didn't,
        the way I see it. I prefer a clean view—
            always have—unencumbered by moral valence; if given
            paper and told to draw morality, I'd draw a cloud
            of meadowlarks when all at once, as if on some cue long ago
    agreed upon,
they disassemble. If most people would draw
a different picture—or say it *can't* be drawn, morality,
    being abstract, as if that meant shapeless (define shape)—
        that doesn't make me wrong or miles ahead of everyone, it
        means I'm not
            someone else, a fact in which I take no little
            pride, though I try to do so humbly, which is to say, in private,
            I keep my best to myself; my worst
    also. I think the truth
lies elsewhere. As with sex, or the weather, or betrayal,
would you rather be surprised, disturbed, bewitched,
    or merely entertained, is maybe
        one way of putting it. Another:

they were men who faltered in front of danger the way
            most men do, who haven't had to live with it. The kind
of men who, having ridden bareback for the first time,
            think they know what it
        feels like, to be a centaur—
the horse's body, the man's
steep chest, all hybridity
    and power, two powers
            especially, lust and intellect, a combination that has
            mostly worked, though we all make mistakes. Right? We
                all do? I know a centaur
            when I see one. These
            were men, riding horses. Absolutely nothing mythological
    about them.

WHEN

WE

GET

THERE

LIKE SO

From attention to adoration
is a smallish distance—

and yet no arrow, no boat
with sail

      can cross it

like the mind's insistence.

We'd reached the marshes, by then, that
all the dead must come to. I could see my face,
tilted there, like a solar eclipse viewed indirectly, which
is the proper way, in a basin of water. You must hold it steady,
keep the basin safe from the wind's reach, its competing
powers of revelation and distortion.

THICKET

Some memories stay,
like fallen throwing-stars
left to lie there; most
disappear, whatever
distinguished them rubbed
smooth by dailiness, glass

into sea glass, from the sea's
tumbling. Like looking
violence for once straight
in the face and watching it
turn, if not gentler, then

differently violent, and
telling yourself that's not
nothing, at least, and

calling it Eros. But violence
has no face. That's just
words into pictures again;
and Eros? Please. You can
make the stars spell out
anything if you stare

long and hard enough:
what part of Didn't you
wish for this aren't you
getting, for example; or

It's a quiet night—quiet,
the way the animals here, east
of touch, but slightly north,
still, of penetration, live
mostly quiet. Most disappear.

Life itself being a ramble of mystery, pattern, accident,
and surprise, we took heart in knowing whatever road we were on
must be the right one—or anyway, we believed it was, and belief
still counts. We pressed forward. We weren't afraid. Nor
unafraid. We stopped briefly to watch the broad leaves,
discolored now, of a catalpa fall onto and get carried
off by the river whose course, more or less,
we'd been following, too. The leaves fell as if to a song called
"Come When I Tell You To," the water
        received the leaves like a slightly different song: "Until
Spoken To, Shut Up, No One's Asking, Did I Ask You
a Question?" Songs like that. Which is how we learned
what we should have known already, that sometimes
to remember a thing can hurt more than the thing itself
ever did, long ago, back when hurt was a feeling, still,
not a memory—not an art, yet. Permission to stop listening, sir,
please. And we turned away, kept heading
wherever-ward, until wherever
became night. How close abundance is to excess, across
whose borders lies too-far-gone-anymore-to-care, a place we'd
        heard about, sure, plenty, but not yet seen.
We made our camp at the border.
The air had turned windless. The trees grew quiet,

like thinking. That animals aren't human, but humans are animals—
it almost sounds like part of a riddle, or the wrong
answer to one, to do as much with obedience as with
what's fair, at least one of us thought but kept, for now, to himself. Variously,
we slept or, in the otherwise dark, pretended to. The only fires we lit
were private ones. Black.
Into blue.

Wave-side, snow-side,
little stutter-skein of plovers
lifting, like a mind

of winter—
                We'd been walking
the beach, its unevenness

made our bodies touch,
now and then, at
the shoulders mostly,

with that familiarity
that, because it sometimes
includes love, can

become confused with it,
though they remain
different animals. In my

head I played a game with
the waves called Weapon
of Choice, they kept choosing

forgiveness, like the only
answer, as to them
it was, maybe. It's a violent

world. These, I said, I choose
these, putting my bare hands
through the air in front of me.

STOP SHAKING

Not the bell, I said—one of us did;
Not the bell, but the smaller sounds, barely noticeable,
trapped inside it. It seemed the kind of thing I might say
to remind myself, when I've forgotten again, what I want
to believe, even now, matters most—precision; though it's hard,
these days, to know for sure what's true. Isn't every season,
no matter what we call it, shadow season? Didn't timothy
use to mean a meadow—a common name, back then at least,

for the sweetest grass? I keep making the same avoidable
few mistakes that I've always made, and then regretting them,
and then regretting them less. Think of all the suffering
happening everywhere, all the time, for nothing.
What if memory's just the dead, flourishing differently
        from how they flourished alive?

MECHANICS

I remember almost nothing now
of who he was, or how I was,
around him. I can make that matter,
or I don't have to, it doesn't
        have to matter,
any more than the small
moth I watched struggling in
what appeared to be—torn and
otherwise empty—an abandoned
web: there was time, yet,
I might have freed it, but even
in abandonment, in what had
        been abandoned—the web,
maybe, but now the moth
for sure—I saw the ghost of purpose
still having a purpose—hard not
to respect that. It's as if
the mind somewhere
        means to shut down memory,
that way preventing us from
understanding too clearly
our own unhappiness, and
in place of memory, offers up
        belief. We believe we're happy.

FIST AND PALM

There are plenty who'd hardly
recognize me now, I used to be
that cruel, by which I mean

I was frightened mostly,
and now I'm mostly not. Joy,
if only flickeringly, each day

astounds me, the man I used to be
dismounts, relents for a bit,
before digging

his boots (streaked
with longing, my own
longing, what I can't help) hard into

my sides again, into the man
I've become, his way of reminding me
we've only stopped for rest,

a short rest,
some water, we've
years to go, still, he has

his job,
I have mine. Speechlessness
is not an option, he whispers

into my ear, he spits
on the words themselves after,
as if to make them stay,

or just to make sure
I'm listening, but I'm always
listening, as I always obey: Isn't this

obedience, these songs I've
built from things too difficult
to speak of?

ON WHY I CANNOT PROMISE

Once, to ring the base of a tree's trunk
meant protection; if the tree died,
or its fruit each year fell too soon,
    then the ring had been somehow
not perfect, or the stones
weren't the right ones; either way,
    protection got confused
with invitation, and what was far,
what we'd hoped to *keep* far, came
    close, settled in: not love, never
mind what it felt like, and not
regret, which I still can't believe in—
    I've tried—and not shame,
which I long ago lost
sight of, though I remember
    waving to it, as it waved
back to me, its slow
wave back, for hadn't the two of us, for
    a good while, been pretty much
unstoppable, even if it hurt inside,
isn't that where hurt
    belongs, Why should you
be different, a question I

still don't get, to be honest. Say the part
    about fear when you're ready to, if you're
ever ready to, you don't have to,
they used to say, sounding
    reasonable, what distinguishes
the second-tier gods
from the first tier. I couldn't think,
    and then I *could* think, but as when
there's only starshine for a light
to go by, does that count
    as thinking: we step away, we can
hear them still rattling—dead leaves—
though we hear from afar.

*how passion
is devoid of
perspective.
intensity
of moments
that will end.
out of breath,
over, now what?*

*I like the
etch'd
in a
pencil
on a
doorframe*

*The ring a tree makes
to mark the year. Does
it want to speed up when
its young or slow down
as it get old. Parched
& faltering the birds
now to heavy to carry
on its shoulder. The
sparton leaves no
longer to provide
shelter from predators*

*Action
to
drama*

*The long ago summers
where kids tried
the big themes of
love, hurt, &
sweat promises
like they were the
only obstacle to
overcome, circumstances
not ever considered
like decay among all this bloom.*

*Names of lovers
etched in bark
long erased,
did you even
remember the
species of
tree you
used to conceal
the topography
of bodies
you would
ravage out
of lust &
pledge
realty to
for a summer.*

*Vehicle for your
wishes,
that tree,
first car,
school--
each ring
that revolves
in our tiny*

47

But that was long, long ago.
Back when lanterns were a real thing
people used, to check the foal's position
inside the birth canal, or for a small boy
to find his way home from shore,
he must have fallen asleep, I can't
see anyone, where did everyone go? He
isn't lost, just a little afraid, but he's
learned how to trick himself into feeling
less afraid: he makes a list in his head
of all he knows for sure. That when
the nights bloom with cricket song,

    not yet, not now

isn't what they're singing, they're
not even singing, it just sounds like that.
How what never happened, if it's
remembered hard enough, can seem
almost true. Nighthawks are called
nighthawks for no fancier reason than
because nocturnal. It was long ago. Now,
as then, there were choices. If not
every choice is one that we get to make,
some we do. You can treat the past
like a piece of fine glass to see yourself
reflected in; or to see through.

GLADIATORS

Each had been terrible
enough to himself
already, to that truest

self, inside, as only he
could know it, so it
seemed it should

matter less what ways
in particular they'd been
terrible to each other,

or even that they'd been
terrible at all. Likewise,
whether death mattered

or not wasn't the point,
had never been, they
understood this, now:

bird crossing sky; sky
getting crossed; the sky
after that . . . They believed,

about suffering,
that its special power
is to define, even as it

displaces it, everything
it touches. They held on
to each other.

CAREER

Long after the dark that the singing was for
is over, some keep singing for a while. As if
refusing to stop could change the fact of daylight

or could make what it felt like to sing hidden
inside the dark—that part, at least—stay. What
is it with the dark, anyway, that the closer they

get to it, the more some people seem to all but
shake with expectancy, even those raised, like us,
to expect nothing?

           —What if all the truth is
is an over-washed sweatshirt, sometimes on
purpose worn inside out?

           *Yet the world's still
so beautiful*, he said. *Sometimes*, I whispered back,
but barely, just in case he was listening; *Sometimes*

it is . . . We were hours from nightfall. Everywhere,
promises kept becoming apologies, our way of
talking-without-talking-about the leaves coming

to rest finally against their own images on the water's surface. It seemed enough, we understood it might have to be, we sat and watched and, briefly, it was.

BACK SOON; DRIVING —

The way the present cuts into history,
or how the future can look at first
like the past sweeping through, there
are blizzards, and there are blizzards.
Some contain us; some we carry
within us until they die, when we do.
The snow falls there, barely snowing,

into a long wooden trough where
the cattle feed on those apples we
used to call medieval, or I did,
for their smallish size, as if medieval
meant the world in miniature but
not so different otherwise from
our own, just smaller, a bit sweeter,
more prone therefore to rot quickly,

which is maybe not the worst thing.
Revelation is not disclosure. I love
how the snow, taking itself now more
seriously, makes the cattle look softer,
for a moment, than their hard bodies are.

REHEARSAL

By then the point of the forest was the getting through it.
Then it lay behind them, all but its sharper details—flies licking at
dried blood, I think, on a random tree stump—getting swiftly lost,
its muffled birdsong, too, that had come less, it seemed, from
the trees than from beneath, mostly, as if somewhere deep,
deep inside the earth. Maybe meeting you has been
the one good reason I lasted so long in a world that must
eventually not include me, I almost said to him. Past the forest,

the shore, where the land ended, where briefly the waves hitting it
seemed the latest example of how squandering momentum can
become routine; while, upon the waves, the taken-for-grantedness
of shadow play seemed its own example: how one way to prove power
can be to quietly assume it. Then except for offshore, where the dark lay
like—defiantly—a ship at anchor, everything was itself. As it always
had been. They took off their shoes, their clothes.
They swam out to the dark ship.

Epigraph: "Now let's sit here for a bit, and stop being sorry about the things we've done" is from *The Birds*, by Tarjei Vesaas, translated from the Norwegian by Michael Barnes and Torbjørn Støverud (Brooklyn: Archipelago Books, 2016).

"Fall Colors": The syntax of the final sentence is indebted to Margaret Noodin's literal translation of an Ojibwe song sung by Gegwejiwebinan, "It is certain they land on me the thunderbirds across my existence." The song appears in *When the Light of the World Was Subdued, Our Songs Came Through: A Norton Anthology of Native Nations Poetry*, edited by Joy Harjo (New York: Norton, 2020).

"Artillery" is built from parts of two poems that originally appeared separately as "Monstrous" in *Ploughshares* and "Silver Bell" in *The Hopkins Review*.

"Little Winter": The question "If someone dreams about you, does it keep you alive?" is from Deborah Eisenberg's story "Merge," in *Your Duck Is My Duck* (New York: Ecco, 2018).

"If Grief Is Mostly Private and Always Various": The final fragment is part of the last sentence of Thomas Wyatt's "Whoso List to Hunt." This poem was commissioned by the Museum of Modern Art (New York) and is in conversation with a photograph in the museum's collection, Michael Schmidt's *Untitled* (nose and lips, pronounced halftone), 1991–94.

ACKNOWLEDGMENTS

Huge thanks to the editors of the following publications, where the poems herein originally appeared, some in slightly different form:

The Atlantic (online): "Gladiators"

bath magg: "Record of Where a Wind Was"

The Fiddlehead: "When We Get There"

Interim: "Searchlights"

Lampblack: "Thicket"

Literary Matters: "Familiar in What Way," "Mechanics," "Yes"

Los Angeles Review of Books: "Vikings"

Magazine (MoMA): "If Grief Is Mostly Private and Always Various"

The Massachusetts Review: "Little Winter"

Michigan Quarterly Review: "On Why I Cannot Promise," "Like So"

The Nation: "Before All of This"

The New Republic: "Surfers"

Ploughshares: "Sunlight in Fog"

PN Review: "Fall Colors," "Heroic Interval," "Rehearsal," "Scattered Snows, to the North"

Poem-a-Day (Academy of American Poets): "Western Edge," "Why So This Quiet"

Poetry: "Back Soon; Driving—," "Regime," "Stop Shaking," "Fist and Palm"

Poetry London: "The Closing Hour," "Troubadours"

Post Road: "This Is the Light"

The Sewanee Review: "Refrain"

ZYZZYVA: "Career," "Somewhere It's Still Summer"